Seasoning

SEASONING

POEMS BY

MARIANNE PHILBRICK

Contents

III. HOME

IV. JOURNEYS

V. SEASONAL SONNETS

VI. RESOLUTIONS

I. EVER
UNHOUSED

FALL OBSERVANCE

What divinity I've found
In storm was blown from branches
To litter autumn ground
With green and prickered pods,

And then was swept away
To collect in city gutters,
Until one sunny day
The husks cracked open

And from each inner membrane,
All rich with moisture white,
The burnished faces came—
The small, resplendent joys.

For God is chestnut brown,
A hard and common seed,
Irregularly round,
Revealed one latter day.

But others, more quick than I,
Would not stop to watch with me
And now, long gone by,
Walk farther down the street.

FEBRUARY 20, 1982

Dreary, the country ice leaks out its hold
On old hills, the deadened heads of grass,
And a first loud chorus of crows calls caustic
And sharp as if to wake the dampened air.
On this day there is no need of hope,
Just the look of soldier lichen, tiny and red
On green squat stems, where stone lets no thing grow.
Love is ever alone, each spring is false:
It is enough two walk, all words forgotten.

FRAME WORK

In winter I have seen this window frame
A space of neutral blue, contain it close
Within the crossing branches of near trees,
And known no chill distance is remote.
I've seen, light lost, the sky a bitter blue,
And each hard line of bark intensely black,
Until, lamp lit, as counterfeit of day,
A single darkness spreads against the pane.
Then fury, fury that heart takes to itself
And cannot put away, that fires and fills
The furrows of the brain and can erode
The soul's geography, is released; is released
To filter shadows of familiar rooms,
And fix each feature as if all were new.

DARK SPIRITS

I'd left the door half-open to catch the breeze,
But a spirit skittered in, was watching me.
It thickened air, grew tentacles that seize,
And pulled me back from what I wished to see.
The house was not my own. I could but sit
Rigid and stiff upon the center chair
While thoughts, like frantic bats closely lit,
Could mesmerize, and as sudden, empty air.
I raised my head, I stood, approached the door,
My hand pushed by the handle, without my will,
And I walked forward once, and heavily more,
Into a land irregular, gray and still;
And now I travel in endless afternoon,
Where day is lost and tomorrow is too soon.

DAY SPIRITS

Brown sparrows peck half-frozen ground beneath
A leafless tree, and brilliant sun, bitter with wind,
Discovers the shops, the faces of shoppers that wreath
The market square, the bustling, busy din,
Until one lone car passes an emptied street.
Round globes on poles shine and know no dark;
While on the corner one mute figure meets
An appointed hour, leaves no accounted mark.
It is then, before morning sweeps down the night—
All is near still—we are about to take
The things of day, let in the window light;
It is then, at some halting thought, we stop, we wait,
Ourselves, alone, upon the vacant air,
And know, invisibly inscribed, the deliberate is there.

SEPTEMBER, 1966

Shall I then eat? This single and dry crumb,
That cannot feed, provides a shattering dread
To make the common all uncommon come
In a lost love that fleshes niggard bread.
Shall I then drink? I can be eased by wine.
But this I see with bare, bald waters mix,
Taking earth's seep, the crushed and blighted vine
To form a drink that clears what mind can't fix.
And if I refuse? I would do well to go,
Stay with those things as certain as they seem,
Discard a knowledge I can never know,
Reject moot promise as a scattered dream.
But the question posed, is asked, again will ask,
And assuming nothing, I assume this task.

FEBRUARY, 1967

I entered one honed corridor of stone,
Where haunted voices hum their hollow chant
And sandaled, harsh heeled feet forever plant
One measured echo within time's rattling moan.
I saw then one high hall where no winds blow
Except to waver winsome candle flames,
And people meet and greet and say my name,
And I, confined, cannot remain, would go
To the brawling street, all odd things rude
Where abrupt winds wind, hail the pitiless need
Of creatures worn by days, or wrapped in greed;
But at sight's dull edge one figure will intrude,
As stoic as rock, more assailable than man,
Who quickly passed, requires I stay and stand.

MARCH, 1967

Too wide a wonder weights the open air.
There, alone, shrill brilliances split the cold,
Confounding the snow-leveled hill. One bare
Persistent twig, gone dry of life is bold.
Here space is caught. The walls forbid frost.
Arched windows filter light. These faces fill
A solitude. In chant is silence lost,
While candles flicker. But light burns still—
These words are black twigs bent to antique type,
Defining loose nature in a reasoned creed
That marks to mind a geometric clarity.
Rich robes are stitched with every shade of light,
And a weight of wonder works in human hands
Which touch, confirm, community and man.

MAY, 1967

No one I know has seen the mountain move.
But winter winds with what wild wail will sing
The bare crest, the lower lines of trees, and prove
Loud herald for the spring's swift watery ring
That retreating snows let slip: it streams, will cross
All paths with liquid color more sharp than the shore.
At the dry edge I kneel, with cupped fingers dip
Down to drink, bring bubbling cold to lips;
But it will not be held, and slips, then pours
Beyond and on, to pool near the wide field;
And fleeing fluid, beneath a leafy shield,
Is still, transparent, deep and settled of dross.
There, lowered down, a burnt and wind-chafed face
Drinks one antidote to thirst, sheer grace.

MARCH, 1982

Then there's another church that's hardly seen.
Confused, uncertain, busy in useless work,
It makes no building, never learned a creed;
There all is futile, except one random mirth.
And with this faint laughter are the dying cheered,
The new-born welcomed, some desperate fed,
The powerful proud accepted, the poor held dear;
And the brave in twos, step down an aisle, are wed.
Somewhere in this foolery, never tidied up,
Of circling clerics in collars, of members entrenched,
Where impasses are passed by decisions to sup,
An enduring frailty is used, cannot be spent:
And there drifts a hope that a halted, thoughtful time
Could speak as from this broke and ancient chime.

FORTY

Lately, uncalled, beauty comes.
I dare not look to see its face.
What I'd have is here at hand
And, quickly, with a liquid ease
Through my fingers runs.
I know, but do not hold;
Ever unhoused, I am at home.

Bitter light no longer blinds,
Eyes are not fractured by what I see.
The lilting bird upon the branch
Will not consume the brain in fire
But lets me pass, walk on.
The flitting feathers discover paths
And I step firm on failing ground.

II. The City

DECEMBER 14, 1964

An ease of snow at evening settled the street;
And done, fast motored wheels spun down black,
As if wrath and force could on a pavement meet,
Powering powder to a perpetual track.
Dazed, I looked aside, found finer lines
Drawn along the walk by two chattering boys,
Who pulled bright sleds and let their voices sign
The air with spreading wisps of spoken joy,
That rising, cloudy, then were caught by cold
Among tall trees; and led all thought to trace
The slim and bending branches as they told
The wind-blown motion of a sky-bound grace.
Soon each twig was faded into night,
And nothing now was darkness, only light.

PRAISE HAVOC

Praise havoc! for spring holes
   In the city street,
Cracked asphalt heaved and opened
   By a swelling earth.

Smooth cement is severed by changing
   Heat and cold
And crumbled by use, by rain
   To a stony mud.

A hard man swings a pick.
   Round shouldered ones
Slow shovel away the debris,
   And pour new tar.

The birds chirrup a chorus,
   As bemused, amused,
Men do the "temporary job,"
   And children watch.

An angry citizen posted
   Red signs of danger,
But the slowing cars, who are passing,
   Feel a sweet breeze.

PARK COMPANION

There was with me once a loneliness
come of a mind crowded with spirits
I could not understand. Each morning
I walked the mental venom out
across the lawns of Frick Park,
skirting the line of trees that wall
the place. At first the grass was green,
then leaves fell and cracked beneath my feet.

One other person, a woman longer
in years than myself, made the same odd circle
just as light flows level and fresh above
the trees. She'd unleash her two black poodles
at the gate, then walk on. She was not hurried,
nor slow; she kept a thoughtful pace.
At times she'd stop; not, it seemed, to look
but to stand quietly the still ground.

One time we spoke: yes, I was new
to the city and a strangeness was here
I'd never thought I'd need to know.
I don't remember what she answered,
only that what I'd said was to her
appropriate, appropriate
when neither I nor the universe

was kind. She left and I stood
to watch the bare wind-whipped trees.

It is not clear to me now when
spring came and I was again too busy
to walk the park. One day remains.
Some snow had fallen in the night.
The sky was dull. A layer of slush
vividly took the other's footprints
as she walked on ahead of me.
I had no wish to stay nor will
to go, but stepped where she had gone.

PITTSBURGH PRIMITIVE

Below the river moves
With a motion too long to see.
One tug pushes the current.
By me whirl cars
On the intricate parkway.
I stand on a concrete island
And look at the other shore.

A steep rise of sandstone
Is touched from here by bridges.
It holds clusters of slim houses
Strung together by roads
Garnished by green trees.
Here a thin permanence, a grace,
Attends me as I pass each day.

The frail walls, narrow, tall
Cling to the rugged hill,
Their clear-eyed windows brilliant
In light-reflecting snow
But clouded, hazed
In the thicker summer warmth
And red smoke the steel mills pour.

They maintain their place,
Home facades for the hands

That fire furnaces below.
There is no third dimension here,
No depth: a height of hill,
A breadth of river bed.
Enough . . . they stand the roar.

KINDERGARTEN IN THE HILL DISTRICT

The Black man came to the empty classroom
Where the teacher waited. Here was work
For his daughter Saronda, the quick mite
Who had no thought, but another pulled
To take her, at once, two different ways.
He was pleased, smiled, and folded each paper
(Someone had embroidered 'Sweet Jesus'
On his white, well-washed overalls).

Their kin had turned them out; she couldn't
Come to school; he had work now.
The teacher saw only the blackboard beyond,
A child who could not draw the white line,
A father's spirit that clawed with bare nails
A surface where he could make no mark
(Someone had embroidered 'Sweet Jesus'
On his white, well-washed overalls).

WAITING

The park at twilight when the people have left:
Greens rustle to nothing, or, like the grass,
Work their unnoticed growth. The times pass.
A still beauty unbeckoning is also bereft.

There's a walk along the museum hall alone
Where ripe peaches on canvas are deep composed
To an echoing order more stern than repose,
But colored to lightness more living than stone.

At the school window the one child stands.
He sees the copter circle searching for smoke.
We remember riots, words cling to our throats
But we clasp: his black, my white hand.

THE LATE EDITION, JOHN GEORGE BROWN (1831-1913)

At Christmas in the Carnegie Library reading room
A red poinsettia on the center table blooms

While we, each beset by book, ceremonial sit,
Continue word rituals of self and another's wit.

The office of turning pages has lulled one man to sleep,
A taut woman spins print with brain in tense retreat.

The air churns active, even, slow and quick: each calls
My thought to one ornate frame upon the farther wall.

There a past-century painter neatly drew young boys
Who, rumpled, pushed to sell newspapers, city employ

To sift the slight, allow the strong, who'd sell—
To later return— buy the street they had worked well.

Lush picture, gift of a gilded Pittsburgh father, now
            benign,
The angular edge is here smoothed out from every line.

We're allowed to see the promise, before the dream came
            gold,
Forget the loss that is better when it is never told.

Now the pictured scene is perfectly altered: below it
        stand
Three slim and simple angels with instruments in hand.

Silent, they say the music which speaking would not
        dare,
While their painted eyes are poised upon no known air.

Bound to the color of the picture by blue and russet dress,
The gilt of their hair is brightened by two candelabra
        pressed

Close to the golden frame. On these, mystic candles
        three
Show father profit, production sums, prosperity.

But what hand has fitted branches—they are evergreen—
To couch the candles, the frame, and fragile angel
        queens?

Christmas at Carnegie Library sees the poinsettia bloom,
And the silent, the evergreen, will creep into the room.

III. Home

LUXURY

Two bundled boys and their dog just grown
Will play the light excess of snow.
Clumsily they run, then plunge
And burrowing, embrace a mass

Of shifting white. This laughingly
They try to hold, then see it flake
From their uplifted hands
To storm again upon the ground.

The puppy flounders, muzzles down,
Pushes crystals up through air
To shine in clear, sky-scouring sun
That lights toy storms with a diamond glow.

Upon the porch the parent stands
Perplexed at what will not be pushed
Away and stay, but breezes back
To fill the paths that go somewhere.

SEPTEMBER 7, 1961

My long steps hurried down the street
To match the short, swift pace of a boy,
Bright smiling beneath a slanting sun,
New clad in corduroy.

I loved the sneakers he wore with ease,
Long scuffed on curbs and grassy paths,
To recall with each light tread
A summer's heat and quiet brooding.

We came to the brick building, a wide door,
The smaller door, and the white list,
Where his name was printed even and black
In its place among the rest.

A teacher stood and spoke to him
And, looking openly in her eyes,
He found nothing brooding there
And went with her to hang his coat.

There along the farther wall
Were shining hooks bright set with coats.
He halted startled by discovery,
Then reached for a place of his own.

I left and a door clicked closed
Behind me, sending a shock
Like the sharp finality of time
To muffle out through the wooden frame.

Restless, I went to work the garden
Earth of weeds, but flowers gone
To seed, made labor useless now.
Then as required, I went to see

Him and others tumble out the door
And, prepared to cheer the day,
I could only return to him
A look, deep sad, within his eyes.

Too quiet to speak, we joined hands
And slowly walked, holding together
One moment more a strong, close season
We had thought was gone.

Our downcast eyes saw feet
Push the dried leaves on a cold street.
We quickened our step and went to buy
The brown, leathered shoes for sharper days.

SAM, THE ZOO MAN

Sam, the zoo man, twelve years old.

Rye Crisp brought for the wet stretched
Noses of elephants;
Silent, he cracks peanuts for himself.

Horror of the lions' roar, caged:
Kept pride of felines and their rowdy cubs;
White polar bears know the cold
A loving element, iced pure.

Seals keep a slippery ease,
And geese stretch their necks to speak.
Ugly is the making of the camel's mouth.
He observes the water level in the dolphin's pool.

There are places in the fence
Where the free get through.
He brings home three feathers:
One brown and russet striped;
One broad, spotted white, and ringed in black.
The last is small, neither blue nor green
But both at once: the peacock's awkward glory.

Sam, the zoo man, twelve years old.

MOTHERING MISPLACED

A wind--winter tinged--
Blows from the north
While a bowed head directs
Mittened fingers to bend
Stark stalks of milkweed,
Sole remaining sentinels
Of autumn-leveled fields.

In breaking them and taking
Them home, I allowed
Silken stranded parachutes
To burst and feather from
Dried and yellowed pods,
And to hang suspended above
A stiff, brown subacid seed.
In this way I prolonged
The last delicate remnant
Of a delicious, departed season.

Indoors, silk and seed
Finally gather on the floor
And I, disgraced, must sweep
Them away to be lost in the
Entrails of man's community.
Outdoors, freeze destroys silk
And nurtures spring-awaiting seed.

WILD ASTER

There are faces I'll not question,
The aster's one of these:
Her proper name I'm not to find,
I just remember she's

Sure to follow goldenrod—
Luxuriant echo of sun—
Obtruding her sparsest purple
When all that's new seems done.

I suppose I could ignore her—
She's not closest to the road,
But her shy eye won't let me past.
She does not think me bold

To pick one of the larger stalks
That stiff, bent once, will break.
Then, easy, I can hand her home,
Set her water glass for drink.

Through the long last work of summer,
My company, she stays.
We would have words, we've much to speak—
But she'd prefer not say

Until her rough and slender leaves,
Her purple stillness, gold core,
Have let my last, my bleached regret,
Grow cold outside the door.

HOUSEHOLD APPLES

I thought of sauce and rows of pie,
And bought a bushel of apples; put them
In the garage, with other good intentions.
I found them later, after a frost:
A few green, unripe ones were firm,
But most lay against each other, brown
And oozing. It would have been right to dump
The lot in a plastic bag for the trash;
But a smell came from them like cider mills
I'd known far away, and wished to remember.
I had no reason to set them out
In the yard, except I've come to think
The open air sympathetic, ready
To receive what all else would disregard.

The odor of apples followed me
When I went to the house, remained in my mind—
An acid-sweet presence, a rich unrest,
Provoking and pensive. I left what I did,
And returned to the yard. The apples were scattered.
Three small squirrels didn't notice me.
They were relaxed and warm in the sun,
Young drunkards, among half-eaten apples,
Insensible of the day, outside
All dimension, at ease, too delighted to play.

Two children came and wanted to hold them;
Things lively and out of reach, and now,
Turned tame. Against my good judgement, I let
One be amiably coaxed to a cage.

The small squirrel, caught, seemed less marvelous;
Was quiet and plain. It was time for lunch.
We ate, and the older boy, the first finished,
Took one piece of sandwich to the squirrel.
He returned to the kitchen, stood silent.
We let him lead us out the door.
A bunch of fur, with taut claws, grabbed
The wire front of the cage. If we came near,
He pulled back, constricted, threw himself
Against the far hard wall and snarled.
"Let him out!" demanded the child.
He disapproved of his mother and squirrel.
I did as he said, then touched his sad face,
Still approving, as always, all uses of apples.

KEEPING TIME

Gift of a father twice great and grand,
The onyx clock, marble based,
Elaborately brass footed, gold faced,
Stolid on our mantle stands.

It was given at a marriage before
My own father was thought of or born.
No one now wishes its weighted form,
But I took it. I cannot ignore

A face made in keeping with time.
We set it to ticking, learned how to wind.
It evenly meters—reliable mind—
Marking our passings with hourly chimes.

The clatter of company covers its sound,
But I waken from darkness, go to the room.
Silent I sit, listen its tune.
Taut involvements are unwound,

Some sturdy thread is collected there,
Is measured out in forgotten pasts;
The freshest feelings are woven, the last
Of some proud pattern embroidered to air.

HOUSEHOLD I

Sun on the surface of this painted porch
Has warmed these steps. It's comfort to my dog,
Who sleeps and does not sleep, and I, who sit
In early summer to think and not to think.
A car intrudes and passes. The noise is echo
To the encircling city, is pulse to me,
A hum of iron and wire that structures the day.

Green argues everywhere. Weeds and grass
Persist against pavement, cracking our paths
With long roots and soft blades. Here is minute variety
More than azalea, roses, and close trimmed hedge.
Above spread ranges of shade, the light and the dark
Of full leafed trees, broad density of maple,
The feminine flutter of the thin decked linden.

Across the street, behind a neighbor's house,
One elm stands closest to the sun. I've seen
It pitch its head in frenzy at the wind
But today, with regal ease, it graceful bends—
I think to bless. Many once arched the street
And, in winter, flashed a blacked domed tracery
Of limbs—signed to vivid air their presence.

Long memory adds presences to day,
Enlivens common hours as I walk the street
And see the swift squirrel jump the power line.
His heart and the humming wire hold that roar
Which lies the other side of silence; each house
Particular holds its place along the street,
And in its place inaudible breaks new sound.

HOUSEHOLD II

Love, it's a wealth of care you've spent on me.
I work alone, but you are present—your presence,
Your present, a cloak of patient, allowing ways.
Sly drafts the leaking earth lets drift are caught
Before they can insinuate my skin.
But no honest shock, no avenue hung with dread
Is now forbidden me. I can go there.
You dress me against the petty fearfulness.

When I see you at my side in early morning—
Your rumpled hair gray upon the pillow—
I know my own flesh is not so sure as once.
And what, forgetting the motion of bared bodies,
If you were not there to curl my toes between
When the fretful covers have fallen in the night?
Would I survive? Without you warm to cloak me
Would I ever step to the fickle floor and stand?

One thought of loss spreads itself to many
Thin strings of memory that can be broken;
And broken, what is done? Who reweaves?
How mend a cloak that time rends hem to hem?
I have seen others lost in loss, a vacuum
Of careless days that they take care to keep
And piece together in a replica dress.
Here warm, I salute all those who go so clothed.

HOUSEHOLD III

There were two sons who now are men.

A time has passed, is now complete.
Between the chatter, the crackers, lost gloves,
There was quiet like the empty street
After the echo stills. It is distant,
But I stop to describe what I do not speak.

Their births were a bounty, little pain.
The only agony, a question:
Could this fragile vigor somehow remain?
It did. They learned to talk, throw stones,
Walk along with others, and complain.

They required of me nothing. We came and went
With the hectic rhythm of make and break.
They maneuvered their blocks, I filled the sink.
We tore out torment in tantrums and glee,
Unwound the day until it was spent.

And always the resonant core. Did we feed
One to the other, the others to one,
As each worked out his own greater need?
Singly we grew, together we drew
One poised and silver sympathy.

There were two sons who now are men.

HOUSEHOLD IV

Our elder son brought you to the closed
Circle within the brick-bound house.
You entered, left one small case in the hall,
And found your way to the living room.

What was your yellow, yellow hair
That threaded a lightness to the day
As space easily bent to receive you?
The tall walls stayed indifferent white,

Later, cold white the frozen lake
When we walked together in the country,
Warm white the woven cap I lent you—
My mother's gift—its fringe of stitching

Bound purple around your head, as you stepped
Unencumbered, alert to the wind.
Your smile, not fierce nor formal, was lovely
As all things time can take, and strong.

You left the cap in your room—it's here.
It's yours, you know, would you return.
It set your head far better than mine.
I missed you when I found you'd gone.

IV. Journeys

HOG ISLAND

Maquashmet Island, for the past hundred years a select
summer colony for wealthy Eastern families, is called by
its original Indian name. In the 18th and late into the
19th century, it was known as Hog Island because
farmers in the area pastured their pigs there during the
warm summer months.
———————————From a Local History

The wind was fair, the waters clear,
Sun showed each threatening rock.
Upon a white and sandy shore
My boat soft pressed and stopped.

I'd come within an endless quiet.
Between the fine green trees
I saw tall houses, kept and trim,
And grasses, gardens neat.

I took a path and then a road,
And at each home I asked,
I knew the ease of inner rooms
Where summer's heat flows past.

The only sound was the bounce of balls
Upon a fenced clay court,
The clink of ice against a glass,
The laughter long and short.

By these strange sounds I have been bound
To slim people on the lawn.
I went to find my little boat
But saw that it was gone.

I knew a causeway there beyond
Could take me to the town.
My feet ran fast on the hot, tarred road—
The bar on the gate was down.

A guard stood watch to check each car
That wished to come that way.
He would not stop someone to leave,
He'd nothing ask or say.

The wind blew harsh, blew loud—
He heard no word I said.
I pressed against the wooden bar,
My heart was hard with dread.

A resident walked near the road,
I asked him how to go,
More raucous blew wild wind around,
His eye was bland and slow.

No hair upon his blond, sleek head
Was stirred by that wind blast,
I caught him by his hard brown arm
And held him long and fast.

He would not speak but made a noise
Like nothing man returns.
I now was dumb, my touch grew numb.
How bright a clear air burns!

A heaviness pressed on my back.
My taut, sure grasp let go.
I ambled to the broad black road,
Walked on so thick and slow.

I came at last to the white, white beach.
A mist spread close on me.
It cloaked the ocean and the shore,
Made mute the sounding breeze.

My foot hit on a wide, washed stone
Where I could sit with ease.
I saw beyond the water's edge
A boulder break the seas

Where cormorants made a slow webbed dance,
Their ragged wings outstretched.
The two stood black, stood still, stood sure,
Then constricted, craned their necks.

I had been told they spread and move
To dry their dampened wings,
But in the haze, and near at hand,
They were a ritual thing.

All dark, all dark they swayed and stood,
A movement dim and deep,
Until, with rapid wings, they climbed
An air both thick and steep.

I remembered—gone my sailing boat---
And now the birds had left
Alone I sat on an empty shore
Not contented, nor bereft.

My feet kicked off my narrow shoes,
My toes clasped at the sand.
How good to sift the tickling grains
Of a firm yet yielding land!

I walk to the edge where waters lap---
Is this a bordered pen?
My eyes grown dim? or is it fog
That walls the shore's long hem?

As sight has shrunk, has my body
Grown gross, fat-bellied, slow?
Do I project a pig's blunt snout
That roots and never knows?

No sound, no sound---I cannot be bound---
Frail fishes each can swim!
This night I watch a misty shore
For images grown dim

That picture the world before I came,
A land of cold and heat
A place that drains down each day's strength,
All faces clash and speak.

The waters wash in an even song,
My stroke is practiced, strong,
Slow arms, the quick fluttering feet
Cross currents short and long.

There can be in that liquid path
A way not seen, unbroken.
It can be passed, it can be made
With a silent, perfect motion.

Take care! the spirits are still near
That marked an ancient sail.
I leave this note where I begin.
I may reach shore, may fail.

BAKER TRAIL

Not frozen, nor at ease with warmth to open,
All autumn leavings split beneath our feet,
As we walked, we four, a trail that touched the rear
Of rural yards, entered deserted parks,
And skirted edges of scarred, shale cliffs.

Once we paralleled a low stone wall
Across a level field. The near horizon
Pressed blank and sunless towards us, held back
By one slim line of black and leafless trees,
Whose feathering branches interrogated gray.

Later, we found a cave that had been a mine,
Abandoned, we thought, to darkness and slow drip.
But, by the entrance, was one wood building
Where we could look between two broken planks
And see a furred, small pony, who, expectant,

Pawed the ground. We were not the ones to come,
And so went on, went on until some ending,
Or brighter days led elsewhere; I'm not sure,
Except, some presence like well-tempered steel
Now reflects each yellow crocus bloom
And sparks in combat with the cut of cold.

SONG

A still land by a deepening sea
I walk in evening light,
When thin-tipped swallow wings
Quiver across my sight.

A flip of forked tail,
The black back will rise.
He turns, and white breast
Is gliding down the sky.

Oh swim the weightless air!
Let burst the crisp cry,
A brittle, swift precision
Where so close the waters lie.

ISLAND

A silent sun had filled the day
Dispersing clouds, becalming wind
Then drinking limpid Time away.

Lake water came against the land
An easy motion on the beach
We heard but would not understand.

Shrill call of swallows broke the air
As swooping, climbing iridescent blue
In frenzy fluttered everywhere.

And pairs so wrought with perfect day
Spun skyward intertwining flight,
Fulfilled the joy they wove away.

And was there lesser ecstasy for two
Who separate sat and with
A single mind thought joy be true?

ENOUGH OF LOVE

Enough of love, enough the laughter,
Never enough these daffodils.
They are not gold, but drunk of sun,
Take light, return it yellow bright,
A color I, blind, may look upon.

Watch then: The few first in a bowl
At home, then go, discover each garden
Where they're alive. Even this will not
Satisfy until I walk the lonely hill
Where the abandoned house is fallen, gone.

Around the sunken cellar hole
New daffodils will nodding grow.
With breeze, they're bowing each to each,
Sweet circle of laughter merrily spirals
A joy more long than the household's love.

MYSTIC, CONNECTICUT: 1775, 1975

Thoughts will not root elsewhere.
They stay by a salt sea shore
Among tall grasses, neglected graves.
There the chiseled stone of Clarissa stands,
Matron and mother. Her children are near,
Round stone markers of the infant dead;
    Sweet lady, did tided waters
    Drain this land's sadness
    And, rising, speak to thee?

Two hundred years out of time
I keep you company, Clarissa,
Planting phantom coffins in earth.
My world is rampant with the living
And I will make no child, although
Allowed a luxury of love.
    Sweet lady, do tided waters
    Drain this land's sadness
    And, rising, speak to me?

NO WILD SWAN STAYS

The wind is bitter.
A lace of last snow is strewn within the woods
Where released streams trickle through bulbed skunk
        cabbage.
Scaly coltsfoot stems begin to rouse a sunny slope.

No wild swan stays.

Lake ice retreats.
A cerulean skirt of water edges an irregular shore,
And upon the narrow liquid rhythm, two swans come,
Fallen from sunny air on whistling white wings.

No wild swan stays.

The two swans ride.
Without force they work new waters, akin to sky and
        ground.
One black beak dips, the first to drink, his privilege
To take, as does his mate, bestowing benediction here.

No wild swan stays.

V. Seasonal Sonnets

THE SEASONS

SPRING: I

Do you know earth weeps when winter's gone?
The fields must lose harsh cold's austere command,
And icy armor shed, proud form reduced
To stubble and mud. Some braver pastures green,
But my feet will falter and sink when I approach
Before assembled seep has worked its course
Through soil's caverns and over the craggy cliffs
In secret, or wailing watery regrets.
The rivers fill and, meeting, more than fill,
Then overflow at sky's electric and loud
Lament, which flails earth's features, until
More gentle rains require a yellow coltsfoot
To sit the rough road sides and I, relieved,
See grief has earned beauty's bright return.

SPRING: II

These are tepid hours, when no green shade
Is grown across the pale, deep-delving sun;
When quiet, unencumbered, stretches out
On empty air, and teases reluctant winds

To brush each face, all faces of a thought,
With a wavering, beguiling, sweet caress.
The green hill warms, and warming sleeps;
Then, sleeping, seems to breathe and slowly wake
To the curt sure peck of a curious bird,
While upon the brown, duff-covered forest floor,
Green spears grow and hang three-petaled-blooms
In a witchery of nodding jocular white,
As around them umbrellas poke and, opening, spread
The fair may apple's fruitful, fatal spell.

SPRING: III

I've seen mere lilacs people a world purple.
So many flowerlets, excesses of scent
Will loll among the blatantly shining leaves,
I consider it duty to pull a blooming branch
From its woody height and break it firmly off;
The venerable hedge regains its sunny height
While I regale my prize within the house.
When darkness comes, at home as out of doors,
Deep redolence is signed to cooling air;
On dampening grasses, as within walls,
Beauty prevails, is breathed as atmosphere.
The frets and fragments of splintering day
Are melded in a rich and deep content,
Forever forgetful that seasons fail.

SUMMER: I

On dull mornings lilies whitely sit the lake,
And I will push my skiff down to the shore,
And row across the inlet to the cove
Where ripples smother beneath green platter leaves,
And dipping oars entangle in slippery stems.
Then I can wait and watch the pointed cups
Of fleshy, rose-ridged blooms, visited
By bees who blackly feed on golden cores
And taste a succulence that's merely scent
To me who stays above the water's depth
And is distracted by a swallow's swoop
That slips a white breast close to water
And then rises, and will take a lilting way
Into a bluing and a brightening sky.

SUMMER: II

The world is green across a rocky brook
And abruptly up the trail where smooth roots
Claw black earth and rock to keep their place
Beneath a distant roof of leaves and light.
The way is level through fewer, straighter trees
Where fronds of fern fall fragrant beneath my boots
Or, nodding, wave me on beyond their ken
To where the boulders show. There one was cleft

Apart and let a single person walk
To a place where light is brilliant just ahead.
There a glade was cut so power lines pass:
I saw above a greater mountain stand;
Then, looking down below, a village was white
Between round trees, the broad and blooming fields.

SUMMER III

Despite opposing winds we sailed to harbor,
Surrounded by gray rock and towering spruce;
We set an anchor, and I was rowed ashore
With those I love, to explore for miracles
That hobble or hole themselves on a sandy beach.
Through air invisible with light, we climbed
On rock to an ancient evergreening wood
Where the youngest slowed and stooped to collect each
          cone
That profligate powers forgetful fling away.
Farther on, a rank but mowed over field
Let us go by a vacant wooden house
That unceasing watched an unceasing sea below,
And there one barren curve of protected shore
Bespoke a sympathy immense, but mute.

FALL: I

What is more delight than aspen trees,
As they shimmer in yellow sun beside the lake;
When wind, like passing errant thought, can turn
Each rounded leaf to a titter of fairy cymbal?
I know no hope they'll stay, for leaves in autumn
Demand a random exit, or, all at once,
Release from a single tree to shroud a field.
Some, just now, careened above the lake,
To become the pristine golden coins
That elegant sit the rippled water, as loss
At first will perch upon the heart's deep calm.
In time they'll drown and brown, be blown ashore,
Where mixed with oak and maple, I will scan
Like tea leaves stranded in a circling cup.

FALL: II

Now that cold hoots the sky hollow,
I see the first of bitter days is back,
And 1 must dress, go out, and with lowered head,
My hands deep down in pockets, pace the leaves.
I have walked a city park, or village path,
And whatever way, when leaves are dried and down,
I find the same vigorous, curt companion.
Among oaks the mood is sonorous,

While ironies crackle from brittle maple leaves;
But whether the day bleed sun or garner clouds,
The hates and pain of all returning frosts
Are said to me and I, then kicking back
With the same crisp tone, am made to smile
And trudge on until, exhausted, I am home.

FALL: III

At last light I scan one level line,
Acknowledge flamboyant fading sun,
And receive a glancing burst from that sharp star
Which sits alone to wait the darkened air.
I more slowly mark the mesh of bare limbed trees
That wind-blown bend, or often undisturbed
Will stand my sentinels until the day
Return to fill their tangled lattices
With morning's level and relieving light.
Slim branches form a screen against the dark.
Ever the blacked spindles across gray sky
Will archly seem to summon deeper night,
And with that arrogant gesture offer me
A sustaining beauty that deigns no sign of hope.

WINTER: I

A scrivener I know keeps company with winter
To exploit a cleansed and bright-lit tablet air.
On coldest days, with one severe, sharp pen,
He limns each twig in our denuded world.
His stroke can score the roofs, the spines of trees,
While bridges done by him more boldly span
Our insolent cliffs; and on the shining days
He can detail a creviced building face
With such a brilliance I am made to wonder
If I have ever come that way before.
Then, at twilight, when he should be done,
I've known him spread the fewest flakes of snow
To swirl, review his work, and require I love
Some lyric he has sketched on dead land.

WINTER: II

Perpetual waves nibble a sullen shore,
Until, ice cold, they increase the thing they touch,
And each lap locks an intricate, whitened lace
To one protruding stone, or dangling twig.
But decor is not enough; a lengthening collar
Is fitted and firmed the endless lake around,
Which wind-swept, broken, torn and set adrift,
Is renewed, rewoven artfully to shore.

At last a whole, completed cloth spreads out
Its ruffled, nubby snows, and severe black depths,
And I can stroll, thoroughly assured
(Where only with craft I could have gone before),
While sun transforms the places where I step
To diamond dazzling carpet, magic as laughter.

WINTER: III

Beside a field of snow and broken stubble
The icy lake persists in waning light,
Except for one low-lapping patch of water
Kept open by a group of migrant birds.
They are one hundred ebony-beaked great swans,
Who strut, on livid land, a lively white,
Or silent ply their pond, where space is shared
With straying coots and very private ducks.
There it was I saw the great wings spread.
Just two engaged the air. They said a whistling,
That repeated, would have recalled the sinking sun;
But no, gone quiet, they steeply circled, returned,
And, crumbling down to ground, both stopped and stood,
Informing me perfection awaited thaw.

SUMMER BROODING

I.

Every air is lidded with one stain,
No sun breaks free across the barest sand
But a green and ragged edge will intervene;
And seeing, I taste that light-gobbling tint
In sugar-tender legumes, carbons bitter;
Or become drunk on salt sea-water verdure,
But tempered by a textured touch of wild mosses,
Low breezes across wide-waving grasses expanding;
All leafage on leafage; wind-swept, inconstant shades
(Where live the devious spirits, imprisoned nymphs),
In a growing imbibed by each breathing simple air
(But closely fenced by village dames in white houses),
And I know the drab-gaudy one inhabits all faces
In a sum of green ways I'd be fearful to own.

II.

Today I watched white water lilies publish
A quiet silence of spreading, pointed petals
Against green sepals and sepals luscious pink
Like light's last retiring flush across the sky.

Because they held about them platter leaves
To still each ripple on their edge of lake,
Each one, with a center yellow eye, maintained
Unflinching gaze at the pulsing, passing sun.
No thing but was motionless, and I looked below
To that twined green world where no light shines
But wavers with slow liquid's brooding logic
And the passage, repose of suspended fishes.
It was then, atop such a world, that the lily
Spice-scented, lotus-like, seemed rightly placed.

III.

Of no note—numberless tawny moth wings,
All beating as if to flame, low about the tree trunks
In a mute tremolo frenzy. But full mating
It proved for the bark-bound, large white females,
When, next year, egg cases broke rife with caterpillars:
Black, sightless, incessant of leg, their enterprise
To climb, inch high in trees, and slide to ground
On shining silk thread, more acrobat than man.
Then an unseasonable falling of scissored leaves,
As wooly mites grew ruby-studded bodies,
Orange carnival heads. Implacable, they jawed
All airy green, and deluged ground with tar turds,
Until a summer's mantle was rendered brown scraps,
And we'd shadeless April drenched with August light.

IV.

When the caterpillars spun cylinder cocoons.
Another greening came. We had not thought
To look, to find it, but it was fully come:
New beech tree suckers perforated lawn
With eerie, parchment leafings. The cloven trunk
Stood tall and brightly silver, now not naked,
But flouncing fair veilings high over roof-tops.
Again we were private from the reaching sun.
Then a single, freshly-minted oak leaf fell
And we had to realize a whole grove new-grown,
Admit new currency had been declared—
Enough to cover earth until next falling off.
It was a bright, pale printing, roughly made,
The unearned interest on our total loss.

V.

The smaller tern is one flutter of pointed parts.
Unable to fly up, but is come down:
Forever he pierces ocean, then catches space,
To bind them both with his shrieking call.
But a winging gull will easy work the air
With even, curving motion; and, gliding, sign
To sky the paths of unseen secret currents

71

Where that severe, glass-eyed bird endures.
But tell me, tell me, how can either of these
Who blue waters ride as on clear blue they rise,
Live the long furies of their home elements:
The changeableness of changing grays and greens;
A firmament riven by light, loudly blasted,
When wide waves menace, meld with a voiding sky?

VI.

"The heated stink, thick sun can choke us,"
I thought, swinging trash bags on the pile;
And done, closed down the car to drive across
The sandy road, as others took my place.
Each dumps his refuse, then tractors level all
To manufacture land composed of plastic wrap—
A soil of all our soils: old melon skins,
Slow oils combining chemicals and rust.
Only the gulls take profit from the broil.
They pull each woeful scrap to know its taste,
And puffed and squawking, let none interfere.
Their numbers grow as they feast feud, attend
Our leavings that no neatness, mechanism, creed
Appears to hide, or make to disappear.

VII.

A road is traveled and the unmoving road
Yet can be said to span and travel too:
With one grasp it's reached from marshy bottom land
Up to a height of rock and lichen hill.
It has traveled once and holds, forever is
The place it's been; while those who come, who go,
Will quickly take, will store in memory
Before a newly passing place is on their eyes.
For some it is no dullness to be place-bound
To one particular stretch; for turning time,
Which unwinds a show of days in equal frames,
Lets nothing occur again that is the same
To those few rooted ones who lonely stay
One hearth and to one other roundly clasped.

VIII.

Whether thick or slim, those trees could rise
In an upward burst against the weight of sky;
And at their height they'd sudden drop their burden
In a finely branched conspiracy of leaves.
No turbulence could arrive to cause dismay,
But became excuse for a sweeping show of grace—
And this if one at random stood the field,
Or many arched our streets in formal quiet.
Now no more are they green. No winter spaces

Are domed by their entanglement of limbs.
Disease has cut them down. Low stumps are left,
Or shining barkless arms that wait to crack;
And we have loving looked the ruddy maple,
Prolific peasant, heavy of shade, sweet blooded.

IX.

Who says a summer's light is never kept?
No, it's saved, in pieces stored, then taken out
And on a dull day watched. What I hold here
Can glitter sulphur yellow, copper red,
Are nearly white or silver gray, and each
Will, iridescent, rattle against its kind.
Small children find them along the ocean shore
And pocket them, bounce them home as jingle shells,
While deep voices decree: bivalve, anomia simplex.
In the look of these shells I ever see sun-specks
Which laughing sparkle on gently wind-touched waters.
In their clatter I ever hear sun-song's
Wry praises for all who catalogue, keep close
One thing fragile, futile, superfluous , and sure.

SPRING LESSON

Winds embroil the thickening branches of tall trees,
And the supple bend, the unsupple splinter down
In dousing rains that rub clear an old day's decay,
As channeled waters whisk out the street's debris.
Then are tepid days of unencumbered light,
When quiet stretches out on endless air,
While the grass hill wakens, rests, and resting
Wakes to the pert hop of curious birds.
These are the last extremes of equinox.
They scour, they ease a lean walled, driven heart
Which waits, as it must, the day without a date,
But a day that certain comes, if uncertain when;
And come, a date ignored, in a dizzy rush.

VI. Resolutions

SWANS

Far from the shore, the old ice split
And a narrow band of rippled blue lake
Opened, signal for the swan's return,
For them to come, at first a double dozen,
Beating rhythmic wings in brilliant light,
And then to stand the ice, ride new water.

It was their flight that wove sun-splintered air
Into an unseen canopy of quiet.
Set down, they stepped the ice and made no mark,
But signed the place as one deliberate,
Now sure, within this time's uneasy web.
Then one alone breasted the water, unmottled,
An effortless, moving grace. When the slim neck
Bent to feed, the niggard snow, the ice, well knew
Their weakened setting was for only this:
A witness to white—perfected, entire, alive.

Of us who watched, of winter failed, the swans
Allowed no notice, but usurped our strength
Into their completed universe; and I knew
It was as well they could not stay, but would
Soon fly to other worlds, their risen wings
Whistling wild song no sound can answer.

THE EXILES

I. Lot's Wife

"Leave now," their only words:
I joined the solemn marchers
Just as darkness tainted day.

Their hooded heads were bowed.
They moved in a steady line.
Only I could see the clouds
Ahead, touched red,
A reflected glow above the desert.

I turned and saw the last sun
Fire my city, enflame
The fixtures of my day
With thoughts that cling and rage
And never will let go.

They left. I am pillared here.
Late I learn to love
What I held, careless, in my hand.

II. Lot

I harrow now a new land:
Seas of green grain
Bend as waves
In the fingering wind,
A full harvest.

I work until the sun dims,
Lessens the pull of the sky
And thoughts that wing too far.

The door to my house
Pushes against emptiness
As it opens.

But the Sword of the Lord
Has carved for me here
A stillness.

The vision was true:
Moisture against thirst,
Grain from harsh sand—
The perfect brilliance encased
In the fruits of labored days.

HAVE YOU SEEN IT BECKON

Have you seen it beckon,
The light of early spring?
It only feeds on what is frail—
Leaves weathered wafer thin,

The random pools new rain has left,
All barest branches poised
Expectant of encircling green,
Lone birds who warble joy.

It's a light to warm a breeze
Nod a painted trillium
Then, like laughter, tumble air.
To think some simple fun

Could check the anger of the wind,
So entirely hold
The arguments of savage winter,
Stultifying cold.

Quiet, it coaxes everywhere
The slightest, greenest shoots,
Trembling gentleness no cold knew.
Who could tell the roots

Would later deep petal a rose,
Send its engulfing scent
To grasp an admiring watcher
Until each wreath was spent?

A PIECE OF TRUANT SUN

A piece of truant sun comes down
Painting Coltsfoot upon gray ground,

And then, not giving up,
Strings long stems for Buttercup;

Later, when summer fills the sky,
I smile for Primrose grown high

Upon stiff stems, and leaning near,
I drink moist scent of lemon here.

Then the heat begins to drain away.
I fear my vagrant friend can't stay,

But he blesses now the slimmest things,
Lets a yellow Lantern wing,

And I, with tenderness forgot,
Stand distant from the Touch Me Not.

And last he charms us against the cold
By plating Rods with endless gold.

For me there are no depths in blue
Nor strength to let the crimson through.

I've no fidelity to green—
A yellow love is all I glean.

A. WYETH

His hands stretch out and, nimble, catch the light
Then force it, for an instant, flood some thing—
The bladed grass, cracked plate, a child's fright:
And a moment, set at the edge of time, will sing.
No clouds confuse thy day, I forget all shadow,
As lines etched on the bare barn door by cold,
Explored, are retrieved from death, and show
We are remotely blessed, perhaps are bold.
Sweet strength of stillness, I will love the dark—
A sputter of bees upon the split ripe pear,
A scent too sweet, a succulence consumed,
A rapture never traced, few pictures mark;
But spent, will work, a honeyed purpose dare;
And feed the dream more deep than flower's bloom.

NIGHT SONG

No wind. The woods are silent.
Cabin walls dissolve in calm.
Far spirits are here.

Come, search the star ceiling:
Silver nails hold darkness
Around us, one glittering dome
(Never seen are the rafters
That bind stars together).

Night has veiled from us
The slight and minute things:
These stir beyond our touch.
Soundless, the leafing argument
Of green, the stoic stone's delay
Seep here close to us,
Enter more near than thought.

There are no feared intruders:
The voices of neighbors were brought
To the hill on vacant air.
We can settle to our house.
Trim sheets are fresh to bared bodies.

Your fond swat, and laughter breaks
The quiet, broken again by clatter
Of ransacking raccoons at play
With tools left out of doors.

The dark of the room thickens
As one body moves to the other.
Our hands press and feel.
Lush pleasing, quickened breath
Spread blood's full rush
Through dissolving flesh
That kneads now each to each.
Deep, past all bounds, two bodies
Arch and grasp a hid beginning
Where joy is opened, and slowly set
In the shadowless arms of sleep.

No wind. The woods are silent.
Elsewhere works the sun
Its passages of light.

NOTES

Fall Observance:

> This poem is apparently one of the first that
> Marianne wrote after her move to Pittsburgh in
> 1962. From that year until 1966, she lived on
> Wilkens Avenue in the Squirrel Hill district of the
> city.

February 20, 1982

Frame Work:

> This blank-verse sonnet is one of several poems
> that Marianne evidently prepared for submission
> to a publisher. Like the manuscripts of the others
> in the group, this one is flawlessly typed, and the
> upper right corner of the sheet bears her maiden
> name and the address of the house where she
> lived from 1967 to 1984 on South Linden Avenue
> in the Point Breeze section of Pittsburgh.

Dark Spirits, Day Spirits

September, 1966; February, 1967; March, 1967; May,
1967:

> These four sonnets mark a crucial turning point in
> Marianne's religious life as she moved from her
> twenty-year fellowship in the Quaker Society of
> Friends to communion in the Protestant Episcopal
> Church.

March, 1982

Forty:

> One of the poems prepared for submission to a
> publisher. Marianne turned forty in 1971.

December 14, 1964:

> Marianne's final revision of this sonnet was made
> in 2013, forty-nine years after she wrote its first
> version. Apparently this was the last occasion on
> which she worked on her poetry.

Praise Havoc

Park Companion:

> Frick Park is the largest of Pittsburgh's municipal
> parks and within easy walking distance from
> Marianne's home.

Pittsburgh Primitive:

> The view is from the Penn Lincoln Parkway
> across the Monongahela River to Homestead and
> the other workers' communities perched on the
> hillside above the steel mills on the far side of the
> river.

Kindergarten in the Hill District:

> The Hill District, just east of the downtown
> center, was one of what were then the two major
> African-American sections of Pittsburgh;
> Marianne taught kindergarten and first grade in
> both. It is the setting of nine of the ten plays

that make up August Wilson's epic cycle of black experience in the city.

Waiting:
The second stanza refers to a still life in the Carnegie Museum of Art in the Oakland district; the third stanza recalls the anxious days of rioting that followed the assassination of Martin Luther King, during which National Guard helicopters circled ominously over the Black neighborhoods of the city.

The Late Edition, John George Brown:
The setting of the poem is the imposing building that opened in 1895 in the Oakland district and serves as the center of the Pittsburgh library system.

Luxury

September 7, 1961:
This is the only poem that relates to Marianne's four years in Burlington, Vermont. The boy is her elder son.

Sam, the Zoo Man:
The setting is the Pittsburgh Zoo and Aquarium in the city's Highland Park, overlooking the Allegheny River. The boy is Marianne's younger son.

Mothering Misplaced

Wild Aster

Household Apples:
> The fondly remembered cider mills were in England's Somerset county, where, as a college student, Marianne worked one summer on a postwar reforestation project sponsored by the Quakers.

Keeping Time

Household:
> All four of the poems in this series are prepared for submission to a publisher.

Hog Island:
> Patterned on Coleridge's "Rime of the Ancient Mariner," this poem is set in a nightmarish version of West Falmouth harbor on Cape Cod, where Marianne's parents shared an inherited summer cottage with other members of their extended family.

Baker Trail:
> This walk through a region of coal mines takes place on the southernmost section of a hiking path that starts just north of Pittsburgh and runs north and west for 132 miles to the Allegheny National Forest.

Song

Island

Enough of Love

Mystic, Connecticut: 1775, 1975

No Wild Swan Stays:
>The typescript is strewn with penciled revisions.
>The setting is Lake Arthur in Moraine State Park,
>north of Pittsburgh.

The Seasons

Summer Brooding:
>This sonnet sequence was written after
>Marianne's move from Pittsburgh to Cape Cod in
>1984. The setting is Barnstable town, where
>Marianne lived in a house on Wequaquet Lake in
>the village of Centerville. In the third and fourth
>sonnets of the sequence, she refers to an
>infestation of Gypsy Moths on Cape Cod in the
>mid-1980s.

Spring Lesson

Swans:
>Like the other poems involving Tundra Swans,
>this one is set in western Pennsylvania.

The Exiles:
>The poem is prepared for submission to a
>publisher.

Have You Seen It Beckon:

The typescript is heavily revised both in pencil and in ink.

A Piece of Truant Sun

A. Wyeth

Night Song:
The setting is a cabin in the woods of Underhill, Vermont, at the foot of Mount Mansfield.

CPSIA information can be obtained at www.ICGtesting.com
Printed in the USA
BVOW06s1833151215

430366BV00019B/246/P